Crème Brûlée

More Than 50 Decadent Recipes

DOMINIQUE AND CINDY DUBY

DEFINITIVE KITCHEN CLASSICS

whitecap

Whitecap Books is known for its expertise in the cookbook market, and has produced some of the most innovative and familiar titles found in kitchens across North America. Visit our website at www.whitecap.ca.

Edited by Julia Aitken
Design by Janine Vangool
Proofread by Erinna Gilkison

Food styling and photography
© 2008 by Dominique and Cindy Duby

Printed in China by 1010 Printing Asia Ltd.

Library and Archives Canada Cataloguing in Publication

Duby, Dominique, 1961–

  Crème brûlée : more than 50 decadent recipes / Dominique and Cindy Duby.

Includes index.

ISBN 978-1-55285-943-8

  1. Puddings. 2. Desserts. I. Duby, Cindy, 1960– II. Title.

TX773.D87 2008   641.8644   C2008-902141-X

The publisher acknowledges the financial support of the Government of Canada through the Canada Book Fund (CBF) and the Province of British Columbia through the Book Publishing Tax Credit.

11 12   5 4 3 2

TABLE OF CONTENTS

CRÈME BRÛLÉE USED TO BE A DESSERT PREPARED ONLY BY PROFESSIONAL CHEFS FOR PAMPERED RESTAURANT PATRONS. NOWADAYS MANY HOME COOKS HAVE A FAVORITE VERSION OF CRÈME BRÛLÉE IN THEIR REPERTOIRES. YOU MIGHT EVEN SAY IT'S NORTH AMERICA'S FAVORITE DESSERT!

The origins of crème brûlée are uncertain but similar desserts have turned up through history in Britain, France, and Spain. Although cooks in ancient Rome were experts at making egg-based dishes, the first mention of crème brûlée appears in a French cookbook in 1661. The Spanish, in turn, have a similar dessert called *crema catalana* which they maintain they invented in the 1700s. The English will have none of this and claim the dessert's creation when, in 1879, a cook at a Cambridge college used an iron displaying the college crest to burn the sugar topping on a custard, calling the dessert "Cambridge burnt cream" or "Trinity cream." In the 19th century, the French translation of "burnt cream"—crème brûlée—came into popular usage in other languages, and probably led many to believe that because of its name, the dessert was uniquely French.

At our company Wild Sweets, whether we're making luxurious chocolates for our Virtual Boutique, writing cookbooks, or researching novel food-science-based projects, we always want to better understand the hows, and more importantly, the whys of cooking so that we can push the envelope of creativity. While everyone's familiar with the time-honored, classic crème brûlée with its vanilla custard tucked under a caramelized sugar topping, there are many variations on this theme, both sweet and savory, and this book explores them all. We've tested all the recipes in our culinary studio to ensure that not only will they work perfectly in your kitchen, but will taste delicious and wow your guests.

Pairing wine with food can be a challenge so we've included a chapter on this too. Classic crème brûlée pairs perfectly with some of the world's greatest sweet wines, including the illustrious French Sauternes and luscious Canadian icewine, but there are other wines which also team well with both sweet and savory brûlées.

We hope our creations will inspire you to add your own flare and invent your very own version of crème brûlée, and that you'll agree with us that these beautiful custards are easy to make, wonderful to eat, and are, indeed, timeless culinary classics.

Crème Brûlée 101

INGREDIENTS

Crème brûlée starts with custard that usually consists of a thickened mixture of milk and eggs. Custards are most commonly associated with desserts or dessert sauces, but they can also be savory. Sweet flans, crèmes caramels, pots de crème, crèmes brûlées, cheesecakes, and savory quiches are all known as baked custards. The same milk/egg mixture cooked over a heat source and thickened or set by the addition of flour or gelatin is called a stirred custard. Depending on how much egg or thickener is used, custards may vary in consistency from a thin pouring sauce to a thick pastelike mixture.

Sweet custards are pretty simple preparations, with the basic recipe using just three ingredients—milk or cream, sugar, and eggs—plus flavoring. Although found in almost every kitchen, these staples come in different forms and the form you choose can make a recipe unique.

MILK/CREAM: Most crème brûlée recipes call for cow's milk, which is generally available in several varieties according to its approximate butterfat content, ranging from whipping cream (35% butterfat) to skim milk (less than 0.5%). If a recipe calls for whipping cream as well as other high-fat ingredients, like chocolate, you can substitute light cream (18% butterfat), which will lower the fat content of the recipe without affecting its taste.

SUGAR: We believe that sugar should be used cautiously and only as needed. A dish that's too sweet is cloying and "tiresome" to our taste buds. So sweeten as you would salt—moderately. Sugar is available in white or brown varieties, granulated fine or coarse, powdered, or even in liquid form, and each adds a different flavor to a crème brûlée.

WHITE SUGARS: Sucrose (table sugar) is the most common sugar and is made from sugar cane or sugar beet. **Fructose** is the sweetest white sugar and is primarily found in honey, tree fruits, and berries. **Glucose** (also called dextrose) is produced commercially from maize, but also from rice, wheat, or potatoes, and is available in solid or liquid form. **Maple sugar** is slightly darker than white sugar and is made by concentrating the sap of the maple tree until the syrup crystallizes. Maple sugar, with its naturally occurring vanilla and caramel aroma notes, is a great alternative to white sugar but it's important to remember that it's noticeably sweeter.

BROWN SUGARS: Brown sugar is a sucrose sugar product (either unrefined or partially refined) with a distinctive brown color due to the presence of molasses (about 3.5% for light brown sugar and 6.5% for dark brown sugar). There are several types of specialty brown sugar available. **Demerara** is a coarse raw cane sugar that takes its name from the Demerara area in Guyana. **Turbinado** (also known as turbinated sugar) is a coarse raw sugar that has been steam-cleaned and has a paler color and more delicate molasses flavor. **Muscovado** (also known as "Barbados sugar") is a type of unrefined brown sugar with a strong molasses flavor and very dark brown color, and is slightly coarser and stickier than most brown sugars.

EGGS: Eggs help to thicken a custard. They're graded according to size and all the recipes in this book were tested with large eggs.

Egg shell color varies according to chicken species or breed (chickens with white earlobes lay white eggs, chickens with red earlobes lay brown eggs). There's no significant link between color and nutritional value.

Unless specifically directed in a recipe, do not whisk eggs excessively but only until all the ingredients are just combined. Whisking eggs too much incorporates air into the mixture and will give the finished custard an airy rather than a dense, creamy texture. Also, make sure that you don't let egg yolks and sugar sit together for any length of time unmixed, as the two ingredients will react and form insoluble particles that are impossible to combine.

Always slowly add hot liquid to cold eggs, not vice versa, and whisk constantly while you pour. We also like to strain custard mixtures through a fine-mesh sieve to ensure the finished custard is completely smooth.

COOKING

CUSTARD: Gentle heat is the key to cooking custards successfully. The simplest way to do this is to bake them in what's known as a water bath. The dishes containing the raw custard are set in a shallow roasting pan, then hot water is added to the pan to come halfway up the sides of the dishes. Although the oven may be at its highest temperature, the water in the pan won't exceed water's boiling point or 212°F (100°C) so the custards won't bake too quickly. A stainless steel pan is best; cast iron and glass retain a lot of heat and are not good choices. Bake the custards uncovered to keep the water temperature more even. Another trick is to place the dishes on a wire rack set in the roasting pan. This allows even water circulation and prevents any water from being trapped under the dishes and coming to a boil.

TORCHING: What makes crème brûlée a *brûlée* ("burnt") is the thin, delicate layer of caramelized sugar on top. After the custard is cooled in the fridge, sugar is sprinkled on top and a few seconds of intense heat is applied. The sugar melts, changes color and flavor, and hardens—so that the serving spoon must shatter through the caramel surface to get at the creamy custard underneath. Alchemy in the kitchen!

Using a torch is highly recommended (see next page). You have the most control this way and you avoid recooking the custard. If you don't have a torch, you can use the oven's broiler element—just make sure your custards are completely chilled. (We suggest placing the custards in the freezer for an hour or so before broiling.) Preheat the broiler to high and broil close to the element; caramelization will take anywhere from 1 to 3 minutes. Whichever method you use, make sure to avoid actual

burning, as burnt sugar is bitter. Move the torch constantly (or if broiling, keep a very close eye on the custards). Note that the sugar will continue to cook for a few seconds after the heat source is removed.

Granulated sugar is easier to work with, but some of our recipes also call for brown sugar. (Any coarser and we suggest mixing it with some granulated sugar.) Before caramelizing, blot the surface of the custard if there are small pools of liquid, and cover the custard completely with sugar. Turn the dishes upside down to remove the excess—you want a thin, even layer so it caramelizes evenly.

EQUIPMENT

Although you can prepare most of the recipes in this book with equipment you probably already have, there are a few specialty items that you may want to add to your kitchen.

BLOWTORCH: Although domestic broilers can caramelize the sugar topping on a crème brûlée, we find using a blowtorch much easier and faster. Handheld torches have an intense, focused flame which is simple to control so heat can be applied quickly and exactly where needed. For kitchen use, a butane or propane torch is best. Look for them in hardware stores and/or specialty kitchen stores.

CANDY THERMOMETER: Since measuring the precise temperature of sugar is so important for our caramel recipes (page 108), a candy thermometer is essential. We prefer the digital versions with remote probes available at specialty kitchen stores.

RAMEKINS: Ramekins are individual heatproof dishes, usually glass, porcelain, or ceramic. They range in size from 2 to 4 fl oz (60 to 125 mL), are round with fluted or ridged exterior sides, smooth, straight inner sides, and a small lip. Ramekins are ideal because they can withstand high oven temperatures as well as the intense heat of a blowtorch or broiler. Their smooth, straight inner sides also make it easy to unmold custards like crème caramel. Choose the shallowest ramekins you can find as in these the heat will be distributed more evenly during baking, reducing the risk of overcooking. Also, for custards that need to be unmolded, a shallower dish produces a dessert that has less chance of losing its shape and spreading if not baked perfectly. Ramekins are readily available in department stores and/or specialty kitchen stores.

SCALE: Although most of the recipes in this book feature volume measurements, we recommend investing in a small weighing scale to ensure accuracy and consistency. Digital scales with 0.1 oz (2 g) increments are fairly inexpensive; look for them in specialty kitchen stores.

SILICONE MAT: Silicone mats and molds provide a completely nonstick surface. They can withstand very high temperatures and are hard-wearing if properly maintained. Their flexibility makes them very easy to work with, and a silicone mat is a must for some of our advanced caramel recipes (see page 108). There are several different brands and sizes of mats and molds to choose from at most kitchen supply stores.

WATER BATH: As mentioned on page 9, custards are best cooked in a water bath. A stainless steel or aluminum roasting pan or cake pan large enough to hold four or six ramekins is best, especially if it comes with a wire rack that fits inside the pan. Check out department stores, specialty kitchen stores, and/or restaurant supply stores for these.

Fruits & Berries

Coconut Brûlée
& Caramel Bananas

COCONUT CUSTARD

1 cup (250 mL) whipping cream

½ cup (125 mL) whole milk

½ cup (125 mL) unsweetened coconut milk

½ cup (50 g) shredded unsweetened coconut, toasted

3 large eggs

⅓ cup (75 g) granulated sugar

2 Tbsp (30 g) brown sugar for caramelizing

CARAMEL BANANAS

3 Tbsp (45 g) granulated sugar

3 Tbsp (45 mL) water

pinch cardamom

3 Tbsp (45 g) salted butter

1 Tbsp (15 mL) dark rum

2 bananas, sliced

GARNISH (OPTIONAL)

Caramel Threads (see page 109)

Preheat the oven to 300°F (150°C).

Whisk together whipping cream, whole milk, coconut milk, shredded coconut, eggs, and sugar in a large bowl.

Using a ladle, divide mixture evenly among 4 ramekins. Place the ramekins in a shallow roasting pan. Pour hot water into roasting pan to come halfway up sides of ramekins. Bake until custard barely moves when ramekins are shaken, or a knife inserted in center of custard comes out clean, about 45 to 60 minutes. Remove ramekins from the roasting pan and let cool at room temperature for at least 45 minutes. Refrigerate for at least 4 hours (overnight is best).

Just before serving, sprinkle brown sugar evenly over custards to cover them completely. Ignite a blowtorch and caramelize sugar until evenly melted, moving the torch constantly so sugar doesn't burn.

Combine sugar, water, and cardamom in a large saucepan. Bring to a boil over medium heat, then cook without stirring until the mixture is thickened and caramel in color, about 5 to 10 minutes. Remove saucepan from heat, stir in butter and rum, then add bananas. Cook, tossing gently, until bananas are evenly coated with sauce. Spoon the Caramel Bananas over the Coconut Brûlée.

Lemon Brûlée & Blueberries

BLUEBERRIES

¼ cup (50 g) granulated sugar

¼ cup (60 mL) water

juice of 1 lemon

1 tsp (5 mL) chopped lemon thyme leaves (optional)

4 cups (450 g) fresh blueberries

LEMON BRÛLÉE

finely grated zest of 1 lemon

⅓ cup (80 mL) fresh lemon juice

½ cup (100 g) granulated sugar

2 large eggs

½ cup + 2 Tbsp (150 g) unsalted butter, softened

2 Tbsp (30 g) brown sugar for caramelizing

GARNISH

4 sprigs lemon thyme

For the blueberries, combine sugar, water, lemon juice, and lemon thyme (if using) in a large saucepan. Cook over low heat, stirring until sugar has dissolved. Increase heat to high, add blueberries, and stir until blueberries are evenly coated with syrup. Immediately transfer to a large bowl and let cool in the refrigerator for 3 to 4 hours.

For the lemon brûlée, whisk together lemon zest, lemon juice, sugar, and eggs in a large heatproof bowl until combined. Place the bowl over a saucepan of hot (not boiling) water, and cook, stirring often, until mixture is the consistency of pudding. Pour mixture into a food processor and let cool slightly. Add butter and process for about 2 minutes or until mixture is thick and creamy and butter has melted.

Using a slotted spoon, divide blueberries evenly among 4 ramekins. Spoon warm lemon custard over blueberries, dividing evenly. Sprinkle brown sugar evenly over custards to cover them completely. Ignite a blowtorch and caramelize sugar until melted, moving the torch constantly so sugar doesn't burn.

Pear Cake Brûlée

softened butter and granulated sugar for coating ramekins

2 Tbsp (30 g) unsalted butter

¾ cup (150 g) granulated sugar

½ cup (125 mL) pear juice

3 large egg yolks

½ cup (125 mL) whole milk

½ cup (125 mL) whipping cream

¼ cup (40 g) all-purpose flour

2 large egg whites

3 Tbsp (45 g) granulated sugar for caramelizing

GARNISH (OPTIONAL)

4 pieces Caramel Paper (see page 111)

Preheat the oven to 300°F (150°C).

Grease 6 ramekins with butter then sprinkle insides with sugar to coat evenly, shaking out any excess.

In an electric mixer fitted with a paddle attachment, beat butter and sugar until creamy. Add pear juice and egg yolks, then beat until the mixture is smooth. Add milk and cream and continue mixing until the mixture is completely smooth. Add flour and mix until just combined. Do not overmix.

In a separate medium bowl and using an electric mixer with clean beaters, beat egg whites until they form soft peaks. Using a rubber spatula, fold egg whites into pear mixture until well combined and no white streaks remain. Divide the mixture evenly among prepared ramekins. Place the ramekins in a shallow roasting pan. Pour hot water into roasting pan to come halfway up sides of ramekins. Bake until lightly golden brown and springy to the touch, about 35 to 40 minutes. Let cool slightly, then turn cakes out of ramekins and let cool in the refrigerator for 3 to 4 hours.

Just before serving, sprinkle granulated sugar evenly over top of each cake to cover it completely. Ignite a blowtorch and caramelize sugar until evenly melted, moving the torch constantly so sugar doesn't burn.

Cranberry Clove Brûlée

1½ cups (375 mL) whipping cream

2 whole cloves

6 large egg yolks

¼ cup (50 g) granulated sugar

¼ cup (60 mL) cranberry sauce

2 Tbsp (30 g) granulated sugar for
caramelizing

GARNISH

¼ cup (40 g) sweetened dried cranberries

3 Tbsp (45 mL) orange liqueur,
such as Grand Marnier

Caramel Threads (see page 109)

Preheat the oven to 300°F (150°C).

Combine cream and cloves in a medium saucepan and bring to a boil over medium-high heat. Remove from the heat, cover saucepan with a tight-fitting lid, and let stand at room temperature for 30 minutes.

Whisk together egg yolks and ¼ cup (50 g) sugar in a medium bowl until well combined. Strain cooled clove cream into egg mixture, then whisk until well combined. Place 1 Tbsp (15 mL) cranberry sauce in base of each of 4 ramekins. Pour cream mixture into 4 ramekins, dividing evenly. Place the ramekins in a shallow roasting pan. Pour hot water into roasting pan to come halfway up sides of ramekins. Bake until custard barely moves when ramekins are shaken, or a knife inserted in center of custard comes out clean, about 45 to 60 minutes. Remove the ramekins from the roasting pan and let cool at room temperature for at least 45 minutes. Refrigerate for at least 4 hours (overnight is best).

Just before serving, sprinkle granulated sugar evenly over custards. Ignite a blowtorch and caramelize sugar until evenly melted, moving the torch constantly so sugar doesn't burn. For the garnish, stir together dried cranberries and liqueur in a small bowl. Cover tightly and leave to soak for at least 2 hours (overnight is best). Top each custard with dried cranberries and scatter with Caramel Threads.

Almond Cherry Brûlée

4 Tbsp (60 mL) whole milk

3 Tbsp (45 mL) whipping cream

1 Tbsp (15 g) almond butter

4 Tbsp (60 g) granulated sugar, divided

2 Tbsp (14 g) custard powder or cornstarch

3 large eggs, separated

1 Tbsp (15 mL) Gelatin Mix (see page 25)

1 Tbsp (15 mL) amaretto liqueur

24–32 pitted cherries (fresh or canned)

GARNISH

⅓ cup (30 g) toasted almonds, coarsely chopped

2 Tbsp (22 g) icing sugar

Combine milk, cream, and almond butter in a medium saucepan and bring to a boil over medium-high heat. Stir together 2 Tbsp (30 g) of the sugar and the custard powder (or cornstarch) in a medium bowl. Whisk in egg yolks until combined. Whisking constantly, slowly add the hot milk mixture. Pour mixture back into the saucepan and cook over medium-high heat, whisking constantly to prevent scorching, until custard thickens and forms bubbles. Remove from the heat and stir in Gelatin Mix and amaretto until combined. Keep warm.

In a medium bowl and using an electric mixer, beat egg whites until foam starts to slide from sides of the bowl and no longer gains volume. Slowly add the remaining 2 Tbsp (30 g) of sugar, beating constantly until egg whites form stiff peaks. Gently fold whites into warm almond custard until well combined and no white streaks remain.

Divide the cherries evenly among 4 shallow ramekins. Spoon custard over cherries, dividing evenly. Ignite a blowtorch and caramelize custard until evenly melted, moving the torch constantly so custard doesn't burn.

Raspberry Vanilla Brûlée

SERVES 4

VANILLA CUSTARD

1 vanilla bean (see note page 32)

1 cup (250 mL) whole milk

3 large egg yolks

⅓ cup (75 g) granulated sugar

2 Tbsp (30 mL) Gelatin Mix (see facing page)

2 Tbsp (30 g) granulated sugar for caramelizing

GARNISH

4 pieces Caramel Paper (see page 111), broken into shards

4–12 fresh raspberries

Split vanilla bean lengthwise and, with the tip of a knife, scrape seeds into a small saucepan. Stir in milk and bring to a boil over medium-high heat. Remove from the heat, cover saucepan with a tight-fitting lid, and let stand at room temperature for 30 minutes.

Using an electric mixer, beat egg yolks and sugar in a large bowl until mixture is pale yellow. With mixer on low speed, slowly add vanilla milk, beating until well combined. Pour the mixture back into a bowl and cook over a double boiler on medium heat until mixture is thick enough to coat the spatula. Do not boil rapidly or custard will curdle. Remove from the heat and stir in Gelatin Mix until combined. Pour the mixture into 4 ramekins then refrigerate until set, about 4 hours (overnight is best).

Just before serving, sprinkle granulated sugar evenly over top of each cake to cover it completely. Turn upside down to remove excess sugar. Ignite a blowtorch and caramelize sugar until evenly melted, moving the torch constantly so sugar doesn't burn.

GELATIN MIX

MAKES 1/4 CUP (60 ML)

¼ cup (60 mL) cold water

1 Tbsp (15 mL) gelatin powder

Combine the water and gelatin in a microwavable container. Allow gelatin to bloom for 5 minutes. Microwave on High heat for 20 to 30 seconds, then let it set at room temperature. Cover the container and store in the refrigerator for up to 1 week.

Strawberry Tart Brûlée

EGG CUSTARD TART

¼ cup (50 g) granulated sugar

¼ cup (60 mL) water

¼ cup (60 mL) whipping cream

1 large egg

¼ tsp (1.25 mL) vanilla extract

four 3-inch (7.5 cm) tart shells, partially baked (homemade or store-bought)

2 Tbsp (30 g) granulated sugar for caramelizing

GARNISH

4 strawberries, sliced

4 sprigs mint

Bubble Caramel (see page 113)

Preheat the oven to 350°F (180°C).

Combine granulated sugar and water in a medium saucepan. Cook over low heat, stirring, until sugar has dissolved. Remove from the heat and set aside to cool. Whisk together cream, egg, and vanilla in a large bowl until combined. Add cool sugar syrup, then stir well. Divide the custard evenly between 4 tart shells, then bake for about 20 minutes or until pastry is golden brown and filling is set (a knife inserted into custard should come out clean).

Just before serving, sprinkle granulated sugar evenly over tart filling to cover custard completely, and turn upside down to remove excess sugar. Ignite a blowtorch and caramelize sugar until evenly melted, moving the torch constantly so sugar doesn't burn.

Apricot Saffron Brûlée

1½ cups (375 mL) whipping cream

2 pinches saffron threads

6 large egg yolks

¼ cup (50 g) granulated sugar

2 Tbsp (30 g) granulated sugar for caramelizing

GARNISH

½ recipe Basic Caramel (see page 109)

½ cup (15 g) unsweetened puffed rice cereal

4 drained canned apricot halves

4 edible flowers, such as pansies, nasturtiums, or violas (optional)

Preheat the oven to 300°F (150°C).

Combine cream and saffron in a medium saucepan and bring to a boil over medium-high heat. Remove from the heat, cover saucepan with a tight-fitting lid, and let stand at room temperature for 30 minutes.

Whisk together egg yolks and ¼ cup (50 g) sugar in a medium bowl until well combined. Strain cooled saffron cream into egg mixture, then whisk until well combined. Divide evenly among 4 ramekins. Place in a shallow roasting pan. Pour hot water into roasting pan to come halfway up sides of ramekins. Bake until custard barely moves when ramekins are shaken or a knife inserted in the custard comes out clean, about 45 to 60 minutes. Remove ramekins from the pan and let cool at room temperature for at least 45 to 60 minutes. Refrigerate for at least 4 hours (overnight is best).

Just before serving, sprinkle granulated sugar evenly over custards to cover them completely. Turn upside down to remove excess sugar. Ignite a blowtorch and caramelize sugar until evenly melted, moving the torch constantly so sugar doesn't burn.

For the garnish, prepare Basic Caramel then quickly stir in puffed rice until well coated. Spread out on a silicone mat or a baking sheet lined with parchment paper. Let cool then break into clusters. Garnish with an apricot half, a cluster of caramel puffed rice, and a flower.

Herbs & Spices

Classic Vanilla Crème Brûlée

SERVES 4

1 vanilla bean (see note)

1½ cups (375 mL) whipping cream

6 large egg yolks

¼ cup (50 g) granulated sugar

2 Tbsp (30 g) granulated sugar for caramelizing

Preheat the oven to 300°F (150°C).

Split vanilla bean lengthwise and, with the tip of a knife, scrape seeds into a medium bowl. Whisk in cream, egg yolks, and sugar until well combined. Using a ladle, divide cream mixture evenly among 4 ramekins. Place the ramekins in a shallow roasting pan. Pour hot water into roasting pan to come halfway up sides of ramekins. Bake until custard barely moves when ramekins are shaken, or a knife inserted in center of custard comes out clean, about 45 to 60 minutes. Remove the ramekins from the roasting pan and let cool at room temperature for at least 45 minutes. Refrigerate for at least 4 hours (overnight is best).

Just before serving, sprinkle granulated sugar evenly over custards to cover them completely. Turn upside down to remove excess sugar. Ignite a blowtorch and caramelize sugar until evenly melted, moving the torch constantly so sugar doesn't burn.

NOTE

You can substitute ¼ to ½ tsp (1.25–2.5 mL) of vanilla extract for the vanilla bean.

Lemongrass Rice Pudding Brûlée

RICE PUDDING

½ cup (50 g) basmati rice

⅔ cup (160 mL) whole milk

1 vanilla bean (see note page 32)

2 Tbsp (30 g) granulated sugar

LEMONGRASS CUSTARD

1 cup (250 mL) whipping cream

1 small stalk lemongrass, trimmed and coarsely chopped

2 large egg yolks

¼ cup (50 g) granulated sugar

1 Tbsp (15 mL) Gelatin Mix (see page 25)

3 Tbsp (45 g) granulated sugar for caramelizing

GARNISH

18 fresh raspberries

6 sprigs mint or lemon balm

Rinse rice in cold water and drain well. Combine rice and milk in a small saucepan and bring to a boil over high heat. Reduce heat to medium-low and cook until rice is tender, about 20 minutes. Remove from the heat. Split vanilla bean lengthwise and, with the tip of a knife, scrape seeds into rice pudding. Stir in sugar. Cover saucepan and set aside.

For the custard, combine cream and lemongrass in a small saucepan and bring to a boil over medium-high heat. Remove from the heat, cover saucepan with a tight-fitting lid, and let stand at room temperature for 30 minutes. Whisk together egg yolks and sugar in a medium heatproof bowl until well combined. Strain cooled lemongrass cream into egg yolk mixture, then whisk until well combined. Place the bowl over a saucepan of hot (not boiling) water, and cook, whisking constantly until mixture is hot, thick, and foamy.

Remove bowl from the heat and stir in Gelatin Mix until completely dissolved. Stir in rice pudding until well combined. Divide mixture evenly among 6 ramekins, then refrigerate for at least 4 hours (overnight is best).

Just before serving, sprinkle granulated sugar evenly over custards. Ignite a blowtorch and caramelize sugar until evenly melted, moving the torch constantly so sugar doesn't burn.

Spiced Bread Pudding Brûlée

1½ cups (375 mL) whole milk

½ cup (125 mL) whipping cream

2 large eggs, beaten

⅓ cup (75 g) granulated sugar

juice and grated zest of 1 small orange

1 tsp (5 mL) vanilla extract

¼ tsp (1.25 mL) ground anise seeds

12 oz (375 g) brioche or challah bread,
cut into ½-inch (1 cm) cubes

¼ cup (60 g) crushed canned pineapple,
drained

1 Tbsp (15 mL) rum

2 Tbsp (30 g) brown sugar for caramelizing

Preheat the oven to 350°F (180°C).

Whisk together milk, cream, eggs, sugar, orange juice and zest, vanilla, and ground anise in a large bowl until well combined. Stir in bread cubes, pineapple, and rum and let soak for at least 30 minutes.

Using a ladle, divide mixture evenly among 4 ramekins. Press on the tops to ensure they're flat and even. Place the ramekins in a shallow roasting pan. Pour hot water into roasting pan to come halfway up sides of ramekins. Bake until custard barely moves when ramekins are shaken, or a knife inserted in center of custard comes out clean, about 1 hour. Remove the ramekins from the roasting pan and let cool at room temperature for at least 30 minutes.

Just before serving, sprinkle brown sugar evenly over custards to cover them completely. Turn upside down to remove excess sugar. Ignite a blowtorch and caramelize sugar until evenly melted, moving the torch constantly so sugar doesn't burn.

Lavender Apricot Brûlée

1 cup (250 mL) whole milk

1 Tbsp (2 g) dried lavender

3 large eggs

¼ cup (50 g) granulated sugar

3 Tbsp (45 g) granulated sugar for caramelizing

GARNISH

6 dried apricots, rehydrated in ½ cup (125 mL) hot water

6 edible flowers, such as pansies, nasturtiums, or violas (optional)

Caramel Nuts made with pistachios (see page 112)

Preheat the oven to 300°F (150°C).

Combine milk and lavender in a small saucepan and bring to a boil over medium-high heat. Remove from the heat, cover saucepan with a tight-fitting lid, and let stand at room temperature for 30 minutes.

Whisk together eggs and sugar in a large bowl until well combined. Strain cooled lavender milk into egg mixture, then whisk until well combined. Divide milk mixture evenly among 6 ramekins. Place the ramekins in a shallow roasting pan. Pour hot water into roasting pan to come halfway up sides of ramekins. Bake until custard barely moves when ramekins are shaken, or a knife inserted in center of custard comes out clean, about 45 to 60 minutes. Remove the ramekins from the roasting pan and let cool at room temperature for at least 45 minutes. Refrigerate for at least 4 hours (overnight is best).

Just before serving, sprinkle granulated sugar evenly over custards to cover them completely. Turn upside down to remove excess sugar. Ignite a blowtorch and caramelize sugar until evenly melted, moving the torch constantly so sugar doesn't burn.

Citrus & Spice Brûlée

1 cup (250 mL) whole milk

½ cup (125 mL) whipping cream

grated zest of 1 orange

grated zest of 1 lemon

1 cinnamon stick

4 large egg yolks

⅓ cup (75 g) granulated sugar

1 Tbsp (10 g) cornstarch

3 Tbsp (45 g) granulated sugar for caramelizing

GARNISH

6 orange and/or grapefruit segments

6 sprigs mint

Combine milk, cream, orange and lemon zests, and cinnamon stick in a medium saucepan and bring to a boil over medium-high heat. Remove from the heat, cover saucepan with a tight-fitting lid, and let stand at room temperature for 30 minutes.

Whisk together egg yolks, sugar, and cornstarch in a large bowl until well combined. Strain cooled milk mixture into egg yolk mixture, then whisk until well combined. Pour mixture back into saucepan and cook over medium heat, whisking constantly, until the mixture thickens. Do not boil rapidly or custard will curdle. Divide the mixture evenly among 6 ramekins. Let cool to room temperature, then cover loosely with plastic wrap and refrigerate for at least 4 hours (overnight is best).

Just before serving, sprinkle a thin layer of granulated sugar evenly over custards to cover them completely. Ignite a blowtorch and caramelize sugar until evenly melted, moving the torch constantly so sugar doesn't burn.

Mint Pistachio Crème Brûlée

¾ cup (100 g) unsalted pistachios

1 cup (250 mL) whole milk

4 large eggs

⅓ cup (75 g) granulated sugar

2 drops peppermint extract

1 cup (250 mL) whipping cream

3 Tbsp (45 g) granulated sugar for caramelizing

GARNISH

1 nectarine, thinly sliced with a knife or mandoline

6 sprigs mint

Caramel Nuts made with pistachios (see page 112)

Preheat the oven to 300°F (150°C).

Put pistachios in a blender (not a food processor). Bring milk to a boil in a small saucepan over medium-high heat. Pour milk over pistachios, then blend on high speed until mixture is creamy and completely smooth.

Whisk together eggs, sugar, and peppermint extract in a medium bowl until well combined. Whisk in cream and pistachio mixture until well combined. Using a ladle, divide mixture evenly among 6 ramekins. Place the ramekins in a shallow roasting pan. Pour hot water into roasting pan to come halfway up sides of ramekins. Bake until custard barely moves when ramekins are shaken, or a knife inserted in center of custard comes out clean, about 45 to 60 minutes. Remove the ramekins from the roasting pan and let cool at room temperature for at least 45 to 60 minutes. Refrigerate for at least 4 hours (overnight is best).

Just before serving, sprinkle granulated sugar evenly over custards to cover them completely. Turn upside down to remove excess sugar. Ignite a blowtorch and caramelize sugar until evenly melted, moving the torch constantly so sugar doesn't burn.

Chai & Milk Chocolate Brûlée

⅔ cup (160 mL) whole milk

2 chai tea bags

1½ cups (375 mL) whipping cream

3.6 oz (100 g) milk chocolate, finely chopped

2 large eggs

2 large egg yolks

2 Tbsp (30 g) brown sugar

3 Tbsp (45 g) granulated sugar for caramelizing

GARNISH

2 Tbsp (30 mL) golden raisins

Caramel Nuts made with pistachios (see page 112)

shaved or thinly sliced fresh young coconut

Preheat the oven to 300°F (150°C).

Combine milk and tea bags in a medium saucepan and bring to a boil over medium-high heat. Remove from the heat, cover saucepan with a tight-fitting lid, and let stand for 30 minutes. Remove tea bags, squeezing out excess liquid, and discard bags. Add cream to saucepan and heat over medium-high heat until almost boiling. Remove from the heat and stir in chocolate until melted and smooth.

Whisk together eggs, egg yolks, and brown sugar in a medium bowl until well combined. Slowly add hot chocolate mixture to egg mixture, whisking constantly until well combined. Divide mixture evenly among 6 ramekins. Place the ramekins in a shallow roasting pan. Pour hot water into roasting pan to come halfway up sides of ramekins. Bake until custard barely moves when ramekins are shaken, or a knife inserted in center of custard comes out clean, about 60 to 75 minutes. Remove the ramekins from the roasting pan and let cool at room temperature for at least 45 minutes. Refrigerate for at least 4 hours (overnight is best).

Just before serving, sprinkle granulated sugar evenly over custards. Ignite a blowtorch and caramelize sugar until evenly melted, moving the torch constantly so sugar doesn't burn.

Ancho Chili
& Dark Chocolate Brûlée

SERVES 6

1½ cups (375 mL) whipping cream

⅔ cup (160 mL) whole milk

1 tsp (5 mL) ancho chili powder

3.6 oz (100 g) 70% dark chocolate,
finely chopped

5 large egg yolks

⅓ cup (75 g) granulated sugar

3 Tbsp (45 g) granulated sugar for
caramelizing

GARNISH

12 fresh or drained canned cherries

6 sprigs mint

6 Caramel Cages (see page 109)

Preheat the oven to 300°F (150°C).

Combine cream, milk, and chili powder in a medium saucepan and bring to a boil over medium-high heat. Remove from the heat, cover saucepan with a tight-fitting lid, and let stand at room temperature for 30 minutes.

Reheat mixture over medium-high heat until almost boiling. Remove from the heat and strain through cheesecloth to remove the chili powder. Stir in chocolate until melted and smooth.

Whisk together egg yolks and sugar in a medium bowl until well combined. Slowly add hot chocolate mixture to egg yolk mixture, whisking constantly until well combined. Divide mixture evenly among 6 ramekins. Place the ramekins in a shallow roasting pan. Pour hot water into roasting pan to come halfway up sides of ramekins. Bake until custard barely moves when ramekins are shaken, or a knife inserted in center of custard comes out clean, about 60 to 75 minutes. Remove the ramekins from the roasting pan and let cool at room temperature for at least 45 minutes. Refrigerate for at least 4 hours (overnight is best).

Just before serving, sprinkle granulated sugar evenly over custards to cover them completely. Ignite a blowtorch and caramelize sugar until evenly melted, moving the torch constantly so sugar doesn't burn.

Nuts & Chocolate

Hazelnut, Chocolate & Espresso Brûlée

SERVES 6

1½ cups (375 mL) light cream

¼ cup (20 g) espresso coffee beans, coarsely ground

⅓ cup (50 g) whole roasted hazelnuts

¼ cup (60 mL) whipping cream

2.6 oz (75 g) milk chocolate, finely chopped

5 large egg yolks

2 Tbsp (30 g) granulated sugar

3 Tbsp (45 g) brown sugar for caramelizing

GARNISH

2 Tbsp (30 mL) crème fraîche flavored with a pinch of cinnamon

grated zest of 1 lemon

Preheat the oven to 300°F (150°C).

Combine light cream and ground espresso beans in a medium saucepan and bring to a boil over medium-high heat. Remove, cover saucepan with a tight-fitting lid, and let stand for 30 minutes.

Put hazelnuts in a blender (not a food processor). Strain espresso cream over hazelnuts, then blend on high speed until creamy and completely smooth. Pour mixture back into saucepan. Stir in cream and heat over medium-high heat until almost boiling. Remove from the heat and stir in chocolate until melted.

Whisk together egg yolks and sugar in a medium bowl until well combined. Slowly add hot chocolate mixture to egg mixture, whisking constantly until well combined. Using a ladle, divide mixture among 6 ramekins. Place the ramekins in a shallow roasting pan. Pour hot water into pan to come halfway up sides of ramekins. Bake until custard barely moves when ramekins are shaken, or a knife inserted in center of custard comes out clean, about 1 hour. Remove the ramekins from the pan and let cool at room temperature for at least 45 minutes. Refrigerate for at least 4 hours (overnight is best).

Just before serving, sprinkle brown sugar evenly over custards to cover them completely. Ignite a blowtorch and caramelize sugar until evenly melted, moving the torch constantly so sugar doesn't burn.

Maple Walnut Crème Caramel

WALNUT CUSTARD

1 cup (250 mL) whipping cream

½ cup (125 mL) whole milk

½ cup (65 g) toasted walnut pieces

¼ cup (50 g) maple sugar or granulated sugar

2 large eggs

1 large egg yolk

MAPLE CARAMEL

1 cup (200 g) granulated sugar

¼ cup (60 mL) water

2 Tbsp (30 mL) maple syrup

1 Tbsp (15 g) butter

1 Tbsp (15 mL) water

GARNISH

1 large ripe nectarine, pitted and sliced or diced

Bring cream and milk to a boil in a saucepan over medium-high heat. Remove from the heat. Put walnuts in a blender (not a food processor). Pour warm cream over walnuts, then blend on high speed until mixture is creamy and completely smooth. Whisk together maple sugar, eggs, and egg yolk in a medium bowl until well combined. Slowly add hot walnut cream to egg mixture, whisking constantly until well combined. Set aside.

For the maple caramel, combine sugar and water in a medium heavy saucepan and cook over medium-high heat without stirring until it turns a golden caramel color, anywhere from 5 to 10 minutes. Remove from the heat and, standing back in case caramel spatters, add maple syrup, butter, and water, carefully stirring with a long-handled heatproof spoon or spatula. Divide caramel evenly among 6 ramekins. Pour walnut custard into ramekins, dividing evenly. Place the ramekins in a shallow roasting pan. Pour hot water into roasting pan to come halfway up sides of ramekins. Bake until custard barely moves when ramekins are shaken, or a knife inserted in center of custard comes out clean, about 45 to 60 minutes. Remove the ramekins from the roasting pan and let cool at room temperature for at least 45 minutes. Refrigerate for at least 4 hours before turning out custards onto shallow rimmed dishes.

Orange & Pecan Caramel Brûlée

SERVES 4

3 Tbsp (45 mL) whipping cream

grated zest of 1 orange

6 Tbsp (90 mL) fresh orange juice

3 large egg yolks

1 Tbsp (15 g) granulated sugar

1 Tbsp (7 g) custard powder

2 Tbsp (30 mL) Gelatin Mix (see page 25)

3 large egg whites

3 Tbsp (45 g) granulated sugar

FOR MERINGUE

2 oranges, peeled and segmented

Caramel Nuts made with pecans
(see page 112)

Scald cream and orange zest and juice in a medium heavy saucepan by heating over medium heat until tiny bubbles appear around the edge and cream is steaming. Remove from the heat.

Whisk together egg yolks, 1 Tbsp (15 g) sugar, and custard powder in a medium bowl until smooth and creamy. Gradually whisk scalded orange cream into egg mixture, whisking constantly until smooth. Strain mixture back into the saucepan and cook over medium-high heat, whisking constantly to prevent scorching, until custard thickens and forms bubbles. Remove from the heat and stir in Gelatin Mix until combined. Keep warm.

Using an electric mixer, beat egg whites on low speed until they hold soft peaks. Turn mixer to highest speed and add 3 Tbsp (45 g) sugar, continuing to beat until egg whites form firm and glossy peaks. Whisk one-third of the meringue into the warm orange cream until well combined. Add remaining meringue and fold in gently with a spatula until well combined and no white streaks remain. Use at once.

Place some orange segments at the bottom of 4 dessert plates or ramekins. Spoon custard over oranges, dividing evenly. Ignite blowtorch and caramelize tops of custards until golden brown, moving the torch constantly so they don't burn. Top with some Caramel Nuts and serve at once.

Peanut Butter Brûlée

4 large egg yolks

¼ cup (50 g) granulated sugar

2 cups (500 mL) whipping cream

½ cup (125 g) unsweetened and unsalted smooth peanut butter

GARNISH

Caramel Nuts made with peanuts (see page 112)

Caramel Threads (see page 109)

Whisk together egg yolks and sugar in a medium heatproof bowl until well combined. Meanwhile, bring cream to a boil in a small saucepan over medium-high heat. Slowly add hot cream to egg yolk mixture, whisking constantly until well combined. Whisk in peanut butter until well combined. Place the bowl over a saucepan of hot (not boiling) water, and cook, whisking often, until mixture is thick enough to coat the back of a spoon, about 10 minutes. Remove bowl from the heat and let cool slightly. Divide mixture evenly among 6 ramekins. Cover loosely with plastic wrap then refrigerate for at least 4 hours (overnight is best).

Chocolate Crème Brûlée

1½ cups (375 mL) whipping cream

⅔ cup (160 mL) milk

3.6 oz (100 g) 70% dark chocolate, finely chopped

1 large egg

5 large egg yolks

⅓ cup (75 g) granulated sugar

3 Tbsp (45 g) brown sugar for caramelizing

GARNISH

3 whole strawberries, halved

6 sprigs fresh mint

Preheat the oven to 300°F (150°C).

Bring cream and milk to a boil in a medium saucepan over medium-high heat. Remove from the heat and stir in chocolate until melted and smooth. Set aside.

Whisk the egg, egg yolks, and granulated sugar in a medium bowl until well combined. Slowly add chocolate cream to egg mixture, whisking constantly until well combined.

Divide evenly among 6 ramekins. Place the ramekins in a shallow roasting pan. Pour hot water into roasting pan to come halfway up sides of ramekins. Bake until custard barely moves when ramekins are shaken, or a knife inserted in center of custard comes out clean, about 60 to 75 minutes. Remove the ramekins from the roasting pan and let cool at room temperature for at least 45 minutes. Refrigerate for at least 4 hours (overnight is best).

Just before serving, sprinkle brown sugar evenly over custards to cover them completely. Turn upside down to remove excess sugar. Ignite blowtorch and caramelize sugar until evenly melted, moving the torch constantly so sugar doesn't burn.

Chocolate, Orange & Candied Ginger Brûlée

1½ cups (375 mL) whipping cream

⅔ cup (160 mL) whole milk

two 1-inch (2.5 cm) pieces fresh ginger

grated zest of ½ orange

3.6 oz (100 g) 70% dark chocolate, finely chopped

2 large eggs

2 large egg yolks

2 Tbsp (30 g) granulated sugar

3 Tbsp (45 g) granulated sugar for caramelizing

GARNISH

1 or 2 oranges, peeled and segmented

4 tsp (20 mL) finely chopped candied ginger

6 sprigs mint

Preheat the oven to 300°F (150°C).

Combine cream, milk, ginger, and orange zest in a medium saucepan and bring to a boil over medium-high heat. Remove from the heat, cover saucepan with a tight-fitting lid, and let stand at room temperature for 30 minutes. Strain cream mixture through a fine-mesh sieve, discarding ginger and orange zest. Return cream to saucepan and heat over medium-high heat until almost boiling. Remove from the heat and stir in chocolate until melted.

Whisk together eggs, egg yolks, and sugar in a medium bowl until well combined. Slowly add hot chocolate mixture to egg yolk mixture, whisking constantly until well combined. Divide mixture evenly among 6 ramekins. Place the ramekins in a shallow roasting pan. Pour hot water into roasting pan to come halfway up sides of ramekins. Bake until custard barely moves when ramekins are shaken, or a knife inserted in center of custard comes out clean, about 60 to 75 minutes. Remove the ramekins from the roasting pan and let cool at room temperature for at least 45 minutes. Refrigerate for at least 4 hours (overnight is best).

Just before serving, sprinkle granulated sugar evenly over custards to cover them completely. Ignite a blowtorch and caramelize sugar until evenly melted, moving the torch constantly so sugar doesn't burn.

White Chocolate & Sesame Brûlée

2 cups (500 mL) whipping cream

4 large egg yolks

¼ cup (50 g) granulated sugar

¼ tsp (1.25 mL) cinnamon

½ cup (125 g) tahini (sesame seed paste)

1 tsp (5 mL) sesame oil

3.1 oz (85 g) white chocolate, finely chopped

3 Tbsp (45 g) granulated sugar for caramelizing

GARNISH

6 strawberries, whole or sliced

Caramel Glass (see page 112), sprinkled with 1 Tbsp (15 mL) toasted sesame seeds just before baking

6 sprigs cinnamon basil

Bring cream to a boil in a small saucepan over medium-high heat. Whisk together egg yolks, sugar, and cinnamon in a large heatproof bowl until combined. Whisking constantly, pour hot cream in a slow steady stream over yolk mixture. Whisk in tahini and sesame oil until well combined. Place the bowl over a saucepan of hot (not boiling) water, and cook, stirring often, until mixture is the consistency of pudding, about 10 minutes. Remove bowl from the heat and stir in chocolate until melted and smooth. Divide chocolate mixture evenly among 6 ramekins. Let cool to room temperature then cover each loosely with plastic wrap. Refrigerate for at least 4 hours (overnight is best).

Just before serving, sprinkle granulated sugar evenly over custards to cover them completely. Turn upside down to remove excess sugar. Ignite a blowtorch and caramelize sugar until evenly melted, moving the torch constantly so sugar doesn't burn.

Chocolate, Fig & Star Anise Brûlée

1½ cups (375 mL) whipping cream

⅔ cup (160 mL) whole milk

2 whole star anise

3.6 oz (100 g) milk chocolate, finely chopped

1 large egg

5 large egg yolks

2 Tbsp (30 g) granulated sugar

6 dried figs, cut into ½-inch (1 cm) pieces

3 Tbsp (45 g) granulated sugar for caramelizing

GARNISH

2 Tbsp (30 g) granulated sugar flavored with a pinch of ground anise seeds

2 or 3 dried figs, cut into ½-inch (1 cm) pieces and tossed in anise sugar

Caramel Nuts made with walnuts (see page 112)

6 sprigs mint

Preheat the oven to 300°F (150°C). Combine cream, milk, and star anise in a medium saucepan and bring to a boil over medium-high heat. Remove from the heat, cover saucepan with a tight-fitting lid, and let stand at room temperature for 30 minutes. Strain cream mixture through a fine-mesh sieve, discarding star anise. Return cream to saucepan and heat over medium-high heat until almost boiling. Remove from the heat and stir in chocolate until melted and smooth.

Whisk together egg, egg yolks, and sugar in a medium bowl until well combined. Slowly add hot chocolate mixture to egg yolk mixture, whisking constantly until well combined. Divide the chopped figs evenly between 6 ramekins. Divide custard evenly among the ramekins and place them in a shallow roasting pan. Pour hot water into roasting pan to come halfway up sides of ramekins. Bake until custard barely moves when ramekins are shaken, or a knife inserted in center of custard comes out clean, about 60 minutes. Remove the ramekins from the roasting pan and let cool at room temperature for at least 45 minutes. Refrigerate for at least 4 hours (overnight is best).

Just before serving, sprinkle granulated sugar evenly over custards to cover them completely. Turn upside down to remove excess sugar. Ignite a blowtorch and caramelize sugar until evenly melted, moving the torch constantly so sugar doesn't burn.

Almond-Roasted Apple Brûlée

SERVES 4

ALMOND-ROASTED APPLES

2 large Granny Smith apples

¼ cup (50 g) packed brown sugar

⅓ cup (40 g) sliced almonds, toasted

1 tsp (5 mL) finely chopped rosemary

CUSTARD

6 large egg yolks

2 Tbsp (30 g) granulated sugar

2 Tbsp (30 mL) apple juice

1 Tbsp (15 mL) Calvados or brandy
(optional)

GARNISH

4 sprigs rosemary

Preheat the oven to 325°F (160°C).

Peel and core apples, and cut into ½-inch (1 cm) cubes. Toss together apple, brown sugar, almonds, and rosemary in a large bowl until well combined. Transfer to a baking sheet lined with a silicone mat or parchment paper and bake for 15 to 20 minutes or until just tender. Remove from the oven and keep warm.

For the custard, whisk together egg yolks, sugar, apple juice, and Calvados in a medium heatproof bowl until well combined. Place the bowl over a saucepan of hot (not boiling) water, and cook, whisking constantly until mixture is hot, thick, and foamy.

Divide Almond-Roasted Apples evenly among 4 ramekins. Spoon custard over top, dividing evenly. Ignite a blowtorch and caramelize custard until evenly melted, moving the torch constantly so custard doesn't burn.

White Chocolate & Green Tea Brûlée

1½ cups (375 mL) whipping cream

½ cup (125 mL) whole milk

2 tsp (10 mL) good-quality green tea leaves

3.6 oz (100 g) white chocolate, finely chopped

4 large egg yolks

2 Tbsp (30 g) granulated sugar

3 Tbsp (45 g) granulated sugar for caramelizing

GARNISH

12–24 fresh raspberries

6 pieces Pulled Caramel (see page 111) stretched into a shape of your choice

Preheat the oven to 300°F (150°C).

Combine cream, milk, and green tea in a medium saucepan and bring to a boil over medium-high heat. Remove from the heat, cover saucepan with a tight-fitting lid, and let stand at room temperature for 30 minutes.

Strain cream mixture through a fine-mesh sieve into a saucepan and heat over medium-high heat until almost boiling. Remove from the heat and stir in chocolate until melted and smooth.

Whisk together egg yolks and sugar in a medium bowl until well combined. Slowly add hot chocolate mixture to egg yolk mixture, whisking constantly until well combined. Divide mixture evenly among 6 ramekins. Place the ramekins in a shallow roasting pan. Pour hot water into roasting pan to come half-way up sides of ramekins. Bake until custard barely moves when ramekins are shaken, or a knife inserted in center of custard comes out clean, about 60 to 75 minutes. Remove the ramekins from the roasting pan and let cool at room temperature for at least 45 minutes. Refrigerate for at least 4 hours (overnight is best).

Just before serving, sprinkle granulated sugar evenly over custards to cover them completely. Ignite a blowtorch and caramelize sugar until evenly melted, moving the torch constantly so sugar doesn't burn.

Sweet Vegetables

Spiced Pumpkin Brûlée

1 cup (250 g) canned unsweetened pumpkin purée

⅓ cup (60 g) light brown sugar, packed

1 large egg

½ tsp (2.5 mL) cinnamon

¼ tsp (1.25 mL) ground ginger

¾ cup (185 mL) light cream

3 Tbsp (45 g) granulated sugar for caramelizing

GARNISH

½ green apple, cored and sliced

toasted unsalted pumpkin seeds

cinnamon, preferably grated

Preheat the oven to 350°F (180°C).

Whisk together pumpkin, light brown sugar, egg, cinnamon, and ginger in a medium bowl until well combined. Whisk in cream until well combined. Divide the mixture evenly among 6 ramekins. Place the ramekins in a shallow roasting pan. Pour hot water into roasting pan to come halfway up sides of ramekins. Bake until custard barely moves when ramekins are shaken, or a knife inserted in center of custard comes out clean, about 30 to 40 minutes. Remove the ramekins from the roasting pan and let cool at room temperature for at least 45 minutes. Refrigerate for at least 4 hours (overnight is best).

Just before serving, sprinkle granulated sugar evenly over custards to cover them completely. Turn upside down to remove excess sugar. Ignite blowtorch and caramelize sugar until evenly melted, moving the torch constantly so sugar doesn't burn.

Parsnip Vanilla Cheesecake Brûlée

4 oz (125 g) parsnips (about 2 small)

1 vanilla bean (see note page 32)

¾ cup (175 g) cream cheese

6 Tbsp (90 g) granulated sugar

juice and grated zest of ½ lemon

1½ Tbsp (15 g) all-purpose flour

¾ cup (175 g) sour cream

2 large egg yolks

3 Tbsp (45 g) granulated sugar for caramelizing

GARNISH

3–6 seedless green grapes, halved

grated lemon zest

Caramel Nuts made with walnuts (see page 112)

Preheat the oven to 300°F (150°C).

Peel parsnips and cut into cubes. Steam over boiling water for 10 to 15 minutes until very tender. Press parsnips through a fine-mesh sieve.

Split vanilla bean lengthwise and, with the tip of a knife, scrape seeds into the bowl of a stand mixer fitted with a paddle attachment. Add cream cheese, sugar, lemon juice and zest, and flour and beat until smooth and creamy. Using a rubber spatula, scrape down sides of the bowl. Add sour cream and parsnip purée and mix until well combined, scraping the sides of the bowl again to make sure the mixture is smooth. Add egg yolks and beat briefly, then remove bowl from mixer and beat by hand with spatula until mixture is completely smooth.

Divide the mixture evenly among 6 ramekins. Place the ramekins in a shallow roasting pan. Pour hot water into roasting pan to come halfway up sides of ramekins. Bake until custard barely moves when ramekins are shaken, or a knife inserted in center of custard comes out clean, about 40 to 50 minutes. Remove the ramekins from the roasting pan and let cool at room temperature for at least 45 minutes. Refrigerate for at least 4 hours (overnight is best).

Just before serving, sprinkle granulated sugar evenly over custards to cover them completely. Ignite blowtorch and caramelize sugar until evenly melted, moving the torch constantly so sugar doesn't burn.

Carrot, Cardamom & Mango Brûlée

3 large eggs

½ cup (125 mL) whole milk

½ cup (125 mL) carrot juice

¼ cup (50 g) granulated sugar

½ tsp (2.5 mL) ground cardamom

2 Tbsp (30 g) brown sugar for caramelizing

GARNISH

1 mango, peeled, pitted, and sliced

4 sprigs fresh cilantro

Preheat the oven to 300°F (150°C).

Whisk together eggs, milk, carrot juice, sugar, and cardamom in a medium bowl until well combined. Divide the mixture evenly among 4 ramekins. Place the ramekins in a shallow roasting pan. Pour hot water into roasting pan to come halfway up sides of ramekins. Bake until custard barely moves when ramekins are shaken, or a knife inserted in center of custard comes out clean, about 60 to 75 minutes. Remove the ramekins from the roasting pan and let cool at room temperature for at least 45 minutes. Refrigerate for at least 4 hours (overnight is best).

Just before serving, sprinkle brown sugar evenly over custards to cover them completely. Turn upside down to remove excess sugar. Ignite blowtorch and caramelize sugar until evenly melted, moving the torch constantly so sugar doesn't burn.

Rhubarb Marshmallow Brûlée

SERVES 4

RHUBARB-STRAWBERRY COMPOTE

2 Tbsp (30 g) granulated sugar

½ tsp (2.5 mL) powdered pectin

⅔ cup (160 mL) rhubarb juice, made in a
juicer with fresh or frozen rhubarb

1 Tbsp (15 mL) lemon juice

8 medium strawberries, hulled and quartered

CUSTARD

1 cup (250 mL) whole milk

4 Tbsp (60 g) granulated sugar, divided

3 Tbsp + 2 tsp (25 g) custard powder or
cornstarch

1 large egg

¼ tsp (1.25 mL) cinnamon

GARNISH

12 large marshmallows, cut in half

Caramel Nuts made with almonds
(see page 112)

For the compote, combine sugar and pectin in a small saucepan. Stir in rhubarb and lemon juice and bring to a boil over medium-high heat. Cook, stirring constantly, until it is reduced by half. Remove from the heat, let cool at room temperature, then refrigerate for at least 3 hours (overnight is best). Just before serving, gently fold in strawberries.

For the custard, scald milk and 2 Tbsp (30 g) of the sugar in a medium heavy saucepan by heating over medium heat until tiny bubbles appear around the edge and milk is steaming. Remove from the heat.

Whisk together the remaining 2 Tbsp (30 g) of sugar, custard powder or cornstarch, egg, and cinnamon in a medium bowl until well combined. Whisking constantly, slowly add hot milk mixture. Strain the mixture through a fine-mesh sieve back into the saucepan and cook over medium-high heat, whisking constantly to prevent scorching, until custard thickens and forms bubbles. Remove from the heat. Divide the mixture evenly among 4 ramekins.

Place marshmallows over warm custard. Spoon Rhubarb-Strawberry Compote in between marshmallows, dividing evenly. Ignite blowtorch and caramelize marshmallows until golden brown, moving the torch constantly so marshmallows don't burn. Top each custard with some Caramel Nuts.

Roasted Yam & Orange Brûlée

ORANGE CUSTARD

1 cup (250 mL) whipping cream

grated zest of ½ large orange

juice of ½ large orange

6 large egg yolks

⅓ cup (60 g) packed brown sugar

ROASTED YAM MOUSSELINE

1 medium yam, peeled

3 Tbsp (45 mL) whipping cream

1.6 oz (45 g) milk chocolate, melted

1 Tbsp (15 mL) maple syrup

1 Tbsp (15 mL) butter, melted

¼ tsp (1.25 mL) cinnamon

2 Tbsp (30 g) brown sugar for caramelizing

GARNISH

12 orange segments

4 sprigs mint

For the custard, preheat the oven to 300°F (150°C). Combine cream and orange zest in a small saucepan and bring to a boil over medium-high heat. Remove from the heat and stir in orange juice. Cover saucepan with a tight-fitting lid and let stand for 30 minutes.

Whisk together egg yolks and brown sugar in a medium bowl until well combined. Strain cooled orange cream into egg yolk mixture, then whisk until well combined. Divide evenly among 4 ramekins, and place in a shallow roasting pan, pouring in hot water to come halfway up sides of ramekins. Bake until custard barely moves when ramekins are shaken, or a knife inserted in center of custard comes out clean, about 45 to 60 minutes. Remove ramekins from the pan and let cool at room temperature for at least 45 minutes. Refrigerate for at least 4 hours.

For the yam mousseline, preheat the oven to 350°F (180°C). Roast yam in the oven until soft (about 45 minutes), peel and purée in a food processor. Bring cream to a boil in a small saucepan over medium-high heat, then pour over yam purée. Add chocolate, maple syrup, butter, and cinnamon and process until smooth. Refrigerate, covered, for at least 2 hours.

Just before serving, sprinkle brown sugar evenly over custards. Ignite blowtorch and caramelize sugar until evenly melted, moving the torch constantly so sugar doesn't burn. Pipe or spoon yam mousseline on top.

Savory

Yukon Gold & Goat Cheese Brûlée

1 lb (454 g) Yukon gold potatoes, peeled and cubed

½ cup (150 g) soft goat cheese

¾ cup + 2 Tbsp (215 mL) whipping cream

⅓ cup (80 mL) whole milk

2 large eggs

2 large egg yolks

freshly grated nutmeg to taste

salt and pepper to taste

¼ cup (20 g) grated Parmesan cheese

2 Tbsp (30 mL) panko or breadcrumbs

2 Tbsp (30 mL) butter, melted

1 tsp (5 mL) finely chopped lemon thyme

GARNISH

1 small leek (white and pale green parts only), thinly sliced and sautéed in 1 Tbsp (15 mL) butter

2 Tbsp (30 mL) Tobiko fish roe

6 sprigs lemon thyme

Preheat the oven to 300°F (150°C).

Place potatoes in a large saucepan of salted water and bring to a boil over high heat. Reduce heat to medium-low and cook until potatoes are fork-tender, about 15 to 20 minutes. Drain well, then press potatoes through a fine-mesh sieve or a potato ricer into a medium bowl. While potatoes are still hot, add the goat cheese and mash with a fork until well combined. Bring cream and milk to a boil in a small saucepan over medium-high heat, then add to potatoes and stir well. Stir in eggs and egg yolks until well combined. Season to taste with nutmeg, and salt and pepper.

Divide the mixture evenly among 6 ramekins, and place in a shallow roasting pan. Pour hot water into the pan to come halfway up sides of ramekins. Bake until custard barely moves when ramekins are shaken, about 30 to 40 minutes. Remove ramekins from the roasting pan and keep warm.

Stir together cheese, panko, butter, and lemon thyme in a small bowl until well combined and crumbly. Spoon about 1 Tbsp (15 mL) on top of each custard. Preheat oven broiler to high. Broil close to element until topping is crispy and golden brown.

Morels & Asparagus with Stilton Brûlée

STILTON GRATIN

⅓ cup (80 mL) whipping cream

¾ cup (75 g) crumbled Stilton cheese

2 large egg yolks

1 Tbsp (15 mL) corn syrup

1 Tbsp (15 mL) white wine

SAUTÉED VEGETABLES

2 Tbsp (30 g) salted butter

1 Tbsp (15 mL) olive oil

8–12 morel mushrooms (or other small mushrooms such as shiitake or chanterelles)

4–8 stalks fresh asparagus, blanched and quartered crosswise

8 grape or cherry tomatoes, broiled

1 tsp (5 mL) lemon juice

salt and pepper to taste

GARNISH

4 slices pancetta, cooked until crisp

Bring cream to a boil in a small saucepan over medium-high heat. Remove from the heat and whisk in cheese until smooth. Whisk together egg yolks, corn syrup, and wine in a medium heatproof bowl, add the cheese mixture, and mix until well combined. Place the bowl over a saucepan of hot (not boiling) water, and cook, whisking constantly until mixture doubles in volume and is pale and thick. Keep warm while preparing Sautéed Vegetables.

Heat butter and oil in a large skillet over medium-high heat. Add mushrooms and cook, stirring often, until tender, about 3 to 4 minutes. Stir in asparagus and tomatoes and toss gently until heated through. Add lemon juice, and season with salt and pepper to taste. Arrange vegetables in the middle of a warm rimmed serving plate. Pour Stilton Gratin around vegetables. Ignite blowtorch and caramelize top of Stilton Gratin until evenly golden brown, moving the torch constantly so gratin doesn't burn.

Insert a few shards of pancetta in between vegetables.

Mushroom, Bacon & Gruyère Brûlée

CUSTARD

1 cup (80 g) shredded Gruyère cheese

3 large eggs

1 cup (250 mL) whole milk

pinch freshly grated nutmeg

salt and pepper to taste

MUSHROOM TOPPING

9 slices bacon, cut into strips
and cooked until crisp

2 Tbsp (30 mL) olive oil

1 large onion, finely diced

12 diced oyster or button mushrooms

salt and pepper to taste

¼ cup (20 g) shredded Gruyère cheese

2 Tbsp (30 mL) panko or breadcrumbs

2 Tbsp (30 mL) butter, melted

1 tsp (5 mL) rosemary

Preheat the oven to 300°F (150°C).

Divide cheese evenly among 6 ramekins. Whisk together eggs, milk, nutmeg, and salt and pepper in a medium bowl until well combined. Divide egg mixture evenly among ramekins. Place the ramekins in a shallow roasting pan. Pour hot water into roasting pan to come halfway up sides of ramekins. Bake until custard barely moves when ramekins are shaken, or a knife inserted in center of custard comes out clean, about 25 minutes. Remove the ramekins from the roasting pan and keep warm while preparing the topping.

Heat 1 Tbsp (15 mL) oil in skillet over medium heat. Add onion and cook, stirring often, until softened but not brown, 5 to 7 minutes. Remove onion from skillet and set aside. Heat remaining oil in skillet over medium-high heat. Add mushrooms and sauté until tender, about 2 to 3 minutes. Return onion to skillet, add bacon, and season with salt and pepper. Toss briefly over medium heat. Keep warm.

Stir together cheese, panko, butter, and rosemary in a small bowl until well combined. Spoon about 1 Tbsp (15 mL) of cheese mixture on top of each custard. Preheat oven broiler to high. Broil, close to element, until topping is crispy and golden brown. Spoon Mushroom Topping over custards.

Crab, Corn & Cheddar Brûlée

½ cup (40 g) shredded sharp cheddar cheese

1 cup (80 g) cooked Dungeness crabmeat

1 Tbsp (15 mL) fresh chives, finely chopped

2 cloves garlic, finely chopped

¼ tsp (1.25 mL) chili powder

salt and pepper to taste

4 large eggs

2 cups (500 mL) whipping cream

CORN TOPPING

2 Tbsp (30 mL) butter

½ cup (70 g) frozen corn, thawed and drained

¾ cup (60 g) cooked Dungeness crabmeat

salt and pepper to taste

½ cup (40 g) shredded sharp cheddar cheese

2 Tbsp (30 mL) panko or breadcrumbs

2 Tbsp (30 mL) butter, melted

1 tsp (5 mL) finely chopped chives

GARNISH

4 tsp (20 mL) Masago fish roe

Preheat the oven to 300°F (150°C).

Stir together cheese, crabmeat, chives, garlic, and chili powder in a medium bowl until well combined. Season with salt and pepper to taste. Divide crab mixture evenly among 4 ramekins. Whisk eggs and cream in a large bowl until well combined. Strain cooled garlic cream into egg yolks, then whisk until well combined. Divide the mixture evenly among ramekins, and place in a shallow roasting pan, pouring hot water in to come halfway up sides of ramekins. Bake until custard barely moves when ramekins are shaken, or a knife inserted in center of custard comes out clean, about 30 minutes. Remove ramekins from the roasting pan and keep warm while preparing the topping.

Melt butter in a medium skillet over medium heat and cook corn, stirring until hot. Stir in crabmeat and cook, stirring until hot. Season with salt and pepper to taste and keep warm. Stir together cheese, panko, butter, and chives in a small bowl until well combined. Spoon about 1 Tbsp (15 mL) of cheese mixture on top of each custard. Preheat oven broiler to high. Broil, close to element, until topping is crispy and golden brown. Spoon Corn Topping over custards, dividing evenly.

Pecorino, Onion & Chorizo Brûlée

CARAMELIZED ONIONS

1 cup (250 mL) sliced assorted onions, such as Vidalia, Walla Walla, OSO, Rio, and Cipollini and/or sliced shallots

2 Tbsp (30 mL) olive oil

2 Tbsp (30 mL) sherry

1 Tbsp (15 mL) aged balsamic vinegar (10 years old or more)

4 sprigs thyme

salt and pepper to taste

½ lb (225 g) cooked chorizo, sliced

CUSTARD

1 cup (80 g) grated aged pecorino cheese

3 large eggs

1 cup (250 mL) whole milk

pinch ground fennel seeds

salt and pepper to taste

PECORINO TOPPING

¼ cup (20 g) grated aged pecorino cheese

2 Tbsp (30 mL) panko or breadcrumbs

2 Tbsp (30 mL) butter, melted

1 tsp (5 mL) finely chopped thyme

For the Caramelized Onions, preheat the oven to 350°F (180°C). Stir together onions, oil, sherry, balsamic vinegar, and thyme in a small roasting pan. Season with salt and pepper to taste. Roast in preheated oven, stirring occasionally, until onions are soft and caramelized, about 35 to 50 minutes. Remove pan from the oven, add the sliced chorizo, and keep warm.

For the custard, preheat the oven to 300°F (150°C). Divide cheese evenly among 4 ramekins. Whisk together eggs, milk, fennel, and salt and pepper in a medium bowl until well combined. Divide egg mixture evenly among ramekins. Place the ramekins in a shallow roasting pan. Pour hot water into roasting pan to come halfway up sides of ramekins. Bake until custard barely moves when ramekins are shaken, or a knife inserted in center of custard comes out clean, about 25 minutes. Remove the ramekins from the roasting pan and keep warm while preparing the topping.

For the topping, stir together cheese, panko, butter, and thyme in a small bowl until well combined. Spoon about 1 Tbsp (15 mL) of cheese mixture on top of each custard. Preheat oven broiler to high. Broil, close to element, until topping is crispy and golden brown. Top each custard with the Caramelized Onions, dividing evenly.

New &
Modern

Vanilla Crème in Caramel Gelée

CUSTARD FILLING

1 recipe Classic Vanilla Crème Brûlée
(see page 32)

CARAMEL GELÉE DISKS

¾ cup (185 mL) water

½ cup (100 g) granulated sugar

¼ tsp (1.25 mL) citric acid

1 Tbsp (15 mL) Gelatin Mix (see page 25)

¼ tsp (1.25 mL) agar powder*

GARNISH

Caramel Dust (see page 110)

* This recipe was tested with DC DUBY
Elements ARGUM (turn to the last page for
information on how to order).

Prepare and bake the custard following the Classic Vanilla Crème Brûlée recipe, making sure to omit the sugar topping. Use 4 ramekins or 1 soufflé dish.

Stir together ¼ cup (60 mL) of the water, sugar, and citric acid in a medium heavy saucepan. Bring to a boil over high heat. Boil (without stirring) until a candy thermometer registers 340°F (170°C) and mixture is medium-dark caramel in color, anywhere from about 5 to 10 minutes. Remove saucepan from the heat and, standing back in case mixture splatters, stir in remaining water with a long-handled spoon. Return saucepan to medium heat and cook, stirring, until all sugar has dissolved.

Pour caramel into a tall, narrow heatproof container. Blend with an immersion blender while slowly adding agar powder. Continue to blend until well combined. Pour caramel back into saucepan and bring to a boil, stirring, over high heat. Remove from the heat and stir in Gelatin Mix until well combined.

Pour caramel into a 10-inch (25 cm) square baking pan lined with a sheet of plastic wrap. Let cool at room temperature until the gelée is set, about 10 to 20 minutes. Using a 3-inch (7.5 cm) cookie cutter, cut 8 to 12 disks. Spoon 2 Tbsp (30 mL) custard in center of half the disks and top with another disk.

Vanilla Ice Crème with Caramel Dust

SERVES 6

1 recipe Classic Vanilla Crème Brûlée (see page 32)

¾ cup (185 mL) skim milk

1.6 lb (700 g) dry ice pellets

1 recipe Caramel Dust (see page 110)

GARNISH

Caramel Paper (see page 111)

Caramel Nuts made with walnuts (see page 112)

Prepare and bake Classic Vanilla Crème Brûlée, omitting the sugar topping. You can bake the custard in 4 ramekins or 1 soufflé dish.

Pour milk into a medium bowl and whisk in baked Vanilla Crème Brûlée custard until well combined. Using a flexible rubber spatula, press mixture through a fine-mesh sieve into the bowl of a stand mixer fitted with the paddle attachment.

Wearing rubber or latex gloves, wrap dry ice pellets in a towel and crush them to a powder using a rolling pin or a clean hammer. It's important that no large pieces of dry ice remain. Beating on lowest speed, add a little of the dry ice powder and continue beating until dry ice has evaporated. Gradually beat in remaining dry ice powder, ensuring each batch has evaporated before adding more.

Increase mixer speed to medium. Sprinkle Caramel Dust over mixture and beat until smooth. Transfer "ice crème" to an airtight container and freeze for up to 24 hours (it is best served the same day).

Scoop ice crème into individual bowls, and top each portion with Caramel Nuts and a few shards of caramel paper.

Vanilla Crème with Caramel Foam

CUSTARD BASE

1 recipe Classic Vanilla Crème Brûlée
(see page 32)

CARAMEL FOAM TOPPING

1¼ cups (310 mL) water

1 cup (200 g) granulated sugar

½ tsp (2 g) xanthan gum*

* *This recipe was tested with DC DUBY Elements XAGUM (turn to the last page for information on how to order).*

Prepare and bake the custard from the Classic Vanilla Crème Brûlée recipe. The sugar topping is optional.

For the Caramel Foam Topping, stir together ¼ cup (60 mL) of the water and the sugar in a medium heavy saucepan. Bring to a boil over high heat. Boil (without stirring) until a candy thermometer registers 340°F (170°C) and mixture becomes a medium-dark caramel color. Note that this can take anywhere from about 5 to 10 minutes depending on your stove and the type of saucepan you are using. Remove saucepan from the heat and, standing back in case mixture splatters, stir in remaining water with a long-handled spoon. Return saucepan to medium heat and cook, stirring, until all sugar is dissolved.

Pour caramel into a tall narrow heatproof container. Blend with an immersion blender while slowly adding xanthan gum. Continue to blend until well combined. Strain caramel through a fine-mesh sieve into a siphon dispenser. Charge siphon with 2 nitrous oxide (N_2O) cartridges and refrigerate for up to 4 days. Just before serving, use dispenser to top each custard with caramel foam. Serve at once.

Vanilla Crème with Caramel Mousse

1 recipe Classic Vanilla Crème Brûlée
(see page 32)

½ cup (100 g) granulated sugar

2 Tbsp (30 mL) water

½ cup (125 mL) whipping cream

GARNISH

Bubble Caramel (see page 113)

Caramel Nuts made with pecans
(see page 112)

Prepare and bake Classic Vanilla Crème Brûlée, omitting the sugar topping.

Stir together sugar and water in a small heavy saucepan. Bring to a boil (without stirring) over high heat. Boil until a candy thermometer registers 340°F (170°C) and mixture is medium-dark caramel in color. Note that this can take anywhere from about 5 to 10 minutes depending on your stove and the type of saucepan you are using. Remove saucepan from the heat and, standing back in case mixture splatters, stir in cream with a long-handled spoon. Return saucepan to medium heat and cook, stirring, until all caramel is dissolved.

Pour hot caramel into a medium bowl and whisk in baked Vanilla Crème Brûlée custard until well combined. Using a flexible rubber spatula, press mixture through a fine-mesh sieve into a siphon dispenser. Charge siphon with a nitrous oxide (N_2O) cartridge and refrigerate for up to 2 days. Just before serving, use dispenser to fill 6 individual serving dishes with mousse. Serve at once.

Spike each mousse with a shard of Bubble Caramel and top with a few pieces of Caramel Nuts.

Warm Vanilla Crème Gelée Brûlée

SERVES 4

1 vanilla bean (see note page 32)

6 large egg yolks

¼ cup (50 g) granulated sugar

½ cup (125 mL) skim milk

1 tsp (5 mL) agar powder*

1 cup (250 mL) whipping cream

1½ tsp (7.5 mL) Gelatin Mix (see page 25)

2 Tbsp (30 g) granulated sugar for caramelizing

GARNISH

Caramel Threads (see page 109)

* This recipe was tested with DC DUBY Elements ARGUM (turn to the last page for more information on how to order).

Line the base and sides of a 6-inch (15 cm) square baking pan with a sheet of plastic wrap and set aside.

Split vanilla bean lengthwise and, with the tip of a knife, scrape seeds into a large heatproof bowl. Whisk in egg yolks and sugar until well combined. Place the bowl over a saucepan of hot, not boiling, water and cook, whisking constantly until mixture is hot and doubles in volume. Set aside.

Pour milk into a tall, narrow heatproof container. Blend with an immersion blender while slowly adding agar powder. Continue to blend until well combined. Pour milk-agar mixture into large saucepan, stir in cream and bring to a boil over high heat. Remove saucepan from the heat and stir in Gelatin Mix until well combined. Whisk in hot yolk mixture until well combined. Pour into prepared pan. Let stand at room temperature until set, about 10 to 15 minutes, then refrigerate for up to 2 days.

Just before serving, preheat the oven to 225°F (105°C). Remove gelée from pan and peel off plastic wrap. Cut gelée into desired shapes, place on a baking sheet lined with a silicone mat, and reheat in the oven for 4 minutes.

Sprinkle some sugar evenly over gelée. Ignite blowtorch and caramelize sugar until evenly melted, moving the torch constantly so sugar doesn't burn.

Vanilla Crème Brûlée Sous Vide

1 recipe Classic Vanilla Crème Brûlée (see page 32)

Preheat a water bath to 190–195°F (88–90°C).

Prepare the custard from the Classic Vanilla Crème Brûlée recipe. (Do not bake. The sugar topping should be omitted.) Using a ladle, divide custard evenly among 4 ramekins. Cover each ramekin tightly with a sheet of food-grade, heatproof plastic wrap, making sure that a perfect seal forms and no liquid can leak. Place each ramekin in a vacuum bag and seal following vacuum sealer directions. Place sealed bags in water bath and cook completely submerged, while agitating the water bath from time to time to prevent "hot spots" from forming. The custard is done when it is set and barely moves when ramekins are shaken, about 50 to 60 minutes.

Transfer the sealed bags from the water bath to a cold water bath and let cool for at least 45 minutes. Refrigerate for at least 4 hours (overnight is best). Remove ramekins from bags and peel off plastic film. Just before serving, sprinkle the 2 Tbsp (30 g) sugar evenly over custards to cover them completely. Ignite blowtorch and caramelize sugar until evenly melted, moving the torch constantly so sugar doesn't burn.

Caramel Recipes

BASIC CARAMEL

Combine all ingredients in a saucepan and cook on high heat (without stirring) until the mixture reaches 340°F (170°C) or turns a golden caramel color. Note that this can take anywhere from about 5 to 10 minutes depending on your stove and the type of saucepan you are using. Remove from heat and use as needed.

½ cup (100 g) granulated sugar

1 Tbsp (15 mL) corn syrup

2 Tbsp (30 mL) water

CARAMEL CAGES

Prepare Basic Caramel recipe as above. Lightly oil the back of a metal ladle. Wearing heatproof protective gloves, fill a parchment-paper piping bag with hot caramel. Pipe caramel over oiled ladle in a lattice pattern, making sure you pipe sufficient lines so the cage is sturdy enough to be removed from the ladle. Let cool, then carefully remove cage from the ladle. Use at once or store in an airtight container and use the same day.

CARAMEL THREADS

Prepare Basic Caramel recipe as above. Wearing heatproof protective gloves, fill a parchment-paper piping bag with hot caramel. Pipe rows of thin lines of hot caramel onto a silicone mat or parchment-paper-lined baking sheet. Let cool, then cut or break caramel threads into desired lengths. Use at once or store in an airtight container and use the same day.

CARAMEL DUST

½ cup (100 g) granulated sugar

2 Tbsp (30 mL) water

2 Tbsp + 2 tsp (40 g) butter

Combine the sugar and water in a small heavy saucepan. Bring to a boil over high heat (without stirring) and cook until a candy thermometer registers 340°F (170°C) and mixture is caramel in color. Note that this can take anywhere from about 5 to 10 minutes depending on your stove and the type of saucepan you are using. Remove saucepan from the heat and, standing back in case mixture splatters, whisk in butter until melted and excess moisture has evaporated.

Pour caramel onto a silicone mat and let cool until completely hard. Break caramel into small shards. Grind shards in a food processor until a fine powder forms. Use at once or store in an airtight container and use the same day.

PULLED CARAMEL

1¼ cups (250 g) granulated sugar

⅓ cup (80 mL) water

2 Tbsp (30 mL) corn syrup

¼ tsp (1.25 mL) lemon juice

Combine the sugar, water, corn syrup, and lemon juice in a large heavy saucepan. Bring to a boil over high heat (without stirring). Boil until a candy thermometer registers 312°F (156°C) and mixture is golden in color. Note that this can take anywhere from about 8 to 15 minutes depending on your stove and the type of saucepan you are using. It is important to remove the saucepan from the heat as soon as this temperature is reached or the caramel will be too hard to pull properly.

Pour caramel onto a silicone mat. As soon as the edges start to cool, fold them toward the center using the mat to lift the caramel. Repeat folding process until caramel is cool and no longer spreads. Wearing rubber or latex gloves, pull caramel into desired shapes. Use at once or store in an airtight container and use the same day.

CARAMEL PAPER

Combine the fondant and glucose in a medium heavy saucepan. Bring to a boil over high heat, stirring at the beginning. Boil until a candy thermometer registers 340°F (170°C).

Remove from the heat, add spice (if using) and mix until well combined. Pour caramel onto a silicone mat and let cool until completely hard. Break caramel into small shards. Grind shards in a food processor until a fine powder forms.

Preheat the oven to 300°F (150°C).

Form the powder into desired shapes on baking sheet lined with a silicone mat (for best results use a template). Bake until powder melts into a thin sheet, about 5 minutes. Let cool, then carefully remove from baking sheet. Use at once or store in an airtight container and use the same day.

* You can purchase fondant and glucose at your local cake decorating supply store.

½ cup (175 g) fondant*

3 Tbsp (60 g) liquid glucose*

1 tsp (5 mL) spice such as cinnamon or freshly grated nutmeg (optional)

CARAMEL GLASS

½ cup (125 g) corn syrup

Preheat the oven to 350°F (180°C).

Dip a 2-inch (5 cm) wide clean paintbrush in corn syrup and paint a rainbow-shaped strip about 4 inches (10 cm) wide on a baking sheet lined with a silicone mat. You can make quite a few strips at a time, but don't bake too many at the same time because they will cool before you get a chance to shape them.

Bake until syrup is a light caramel color, about 5 minutes. Let cool for about 30 seconds, then carefully remove warm caramel with a spatula and mold into a funky shape. Let cool completely. Use at once or store in an airtight container and use the same day.

CARAMEL NUTS

⅓ cup (75 g) granulated sugar

¼ cup (60 mL) water

3.6 oz (100 g) unsalted nuts, such as almonds, pecans, pistachios, or walnuts

Preheat the oven to 350°F (180°C).

Bring sugar, water, and nuts to a boil in a small saucepan over high heat. Boil for 2 minutes, then strain through a fine-mesh sieve, discarding liquid.

Spread nuts on a baking sheet lined with a silicone mat or parchment paper and bake until golden brown, about 10 to 15 minutes. Let cool completely, then store in an airtight container.

BUBBLE CARAMEL

Line a rimless baking sheet with parchment paper or invert a rimmed baking sheet and lay paper on base. Combine together sugar, water, and corn syrup in a medium heavy saucepan. Bring to a boil over high heat (without stirring) and cook until a candy thermometer registers 312°F (156°C). Note that this can take anywhere from about 5 to 10 minutes depending on your stove and the type of saucepan you are using.

Brush or spray parchment paper with alcohol. Pour caramel onto one end of paper, leaving a 2-inch (5 cm) border so you can grasp the paper. Hold the caramel end of the paper and hold it up so that caramel starts to run down toward the other end forming a thin, even sheet. Let cool until completely hard, then break into desired shapes. Use at once or store in an airtight container and use the same day. Depending on the size of your baking sheet, you may have to form the Bubble Caramel in batches.

¾ cup (150 g) granulated sugar

3 Tbsp (45 mL) water

1 Tbsp (15 mL) corn syrup

clear alcohol, such as vodka, white rum, or gin

Designing Your Own Crème Brûlée

Don't let yourself be confined by predictable flavor combinations. Expand your culinary horizons by experimenting with crème brûlée recipes. It's easier than you think to come up with a new version of crème brûlée that is custom-made for your taste buds. And remember: experimentation is the key to new discoveries!

We've provided some wonderful flavor combinations to inspire you. Many of these combinations come from recipes that we designed over the years, but several of them have been inspired by various restaurant menus that we've seen during our travels.

Keep in mind that these are suggestions only. For example, we experimented a lot with saffron and apricots as a flavor combination in our Wild Sweets chocolate boutique atelier with great success. However, if you don't like apricots or they are out of season, use nectarines instead. Or if you don't enjoy saffron, try vanilla or ginger; they work very well with apricots.

After choosing the flavors and ingredients you'd like to use, see the *Quantities Chart* (next page) to determine how much of each ingredient you'll need. Then make the basic custard recipe following the guidelines provided. Note that cooking time and results will vary depending on your ingredients. Experiment to determine what works for you.

QUANTITIES CHART

Note that these measurements are not intended to be taken as precise, but rather provided as a guideline. We recommend that you start with a smaller amount than suggested and increase that amount, if you'd like. Remember that you can always add more, but you cannot reduce or take away once it is added to the recipe.

INGREDIENT	RECIPE STEP	QUANTITY
Chocolate		
dark chocolate (>60%)	step 1	*2 oz (60 g)*
milk chocolate (>34%)	step 1	*2 oz (60 g)*
white chocolate (>30%)	step 1	*2 oz (60 g)*
Coffee		
dark roast coffee, ground	step 1: infusion	*¼ cup (20 g)*
instant coffee	step 1	*1 Tbsp (15 mL)*
Extract		
liquid extract— vanilla, bitter almond, lemon, etc.	step 3	*¼ to ½ tsp (1.25 to 2.5 mL)*
Fruit		
dried, rehydrated, or squeezed fruit— figs, apricots, cherries, dates, etc.	step 3	*¼ to ½ cup (60 to 125 g)*
fresh or cooked fruit, chopped or puréed— bananas, apples, pears, etc.	step 3	*1 whole*
fruit juice concentrate—orange, grape, apple, etc.	step 1: aroma	*1 to 2 Tbsp (15 to 30 mL)*
fruit syrup—grenadine, cassis, grape, etc.	step 3	*2 tsp (10 mL)*
fruit zest—orange, lime, lemon, grapefruit, etc.	step 1: aroma	*1 tsp (5 mL)*

INGREDIENT	RECIPE STEP	QUANTITY
Herbs		
stalks—thyme, rosemary, lemongrass, etc.	step 1: infusion	*1 to 4 sprigs*
leaves—basil, tarragon, mint, lemon verbena, lemon balm, lavender, kaffir lime leaf, etc.	step 1: infusion	*½ to 1 tsp (2.5 to 5 mL)*
Liqueur		
20% alcohol or higher—Grand Marnier, Kahlúa, Benedictine, sambuca, Frangelico, amaretto, etc.	step 3	*1 to 2 Tbsp (15 to 30 mL)*
Nuts and Seeds		
nut milk—coconut, walnut, hazelnut, almond, etc.	step 3	*20% of total liquid*
nuts, whole—almond, hazelnut, etc.	step 1	*¼ cup (60 g)*
nut or seed butter—peanut, almond, hazelnut, sesame, sunflower, etc.	step 3	*¼ cup (60 g)*
Spice		
ground, powdered spice—cinnamon, ginger, cardamom, sweet curry, garam masala, allspice, clove, nutmeg, pepper, cassia, mace, grain of paradise, ras el hanout, etc.	step 1: aroma	*¼ to ¾ tsp (1.25 to 3.75 mL)*
other spices—saffron	step 1: aroma	*pinch*
seeds—fennel, anise, coriander, chicory, etc.	step 1: infusion	*1 Tbsp (15 mL)*
whole spices and stalks—cinnamon, vanilla, licorice, star anise, tamarind, etc.	step 1: infusion	*1 whole*
Vegetables		
canned and/or puréed vegetables—pumpkin, sweet potato, yam, parsnip, etc.	step 3	*¼ to ½ cup (60 to 125 g)*
Wine		
sweet and fortified wine—port, Sauternes, etc.	step 3	*1 to 2 Tbsp (15 to 30 mL)*

Basic Crème Brûlée Recipe

SERVES 4-6

1½ cups (375 mL) whipping cream

6 large egg yolks

¼ cup (50 g) granulated sugar

2 Tbsp (30 g) granulated sugar for caramelizing

Preheat the oven to 300°F (150°C).

STEP 1

If using an infusion: Combine whipping cream and infusion ingredient in a medium saucepan, and bring to a boil over medium-high heat. Remove from the heat, cover saucepan with a tight-fitting lid, and let stand at room temperature for 30 minutes. Strain before adding to egg mixture.

If using nuts: Put nuts in a blender (not a food processor). Bring whipping cream to a boil in a small saucepan over medium-high heat. Pour whipping cream over nuts, then blend on high speed until mixture is creamy and completely smooth.

If using aromas, chocolate, or instant coffee: Add to the cream now and combine until the aroma, chocolate, or instant coffee is melted or the mixture is smooth.

STEP 2

Whisk together egg yolks and ¼ cup (50 g) sugar in a medium bowl until well combined. Slowly add whipping cream into egg mixture, then whisk until well combined.

STEP 3

If using dried or fresh fruit, fruit syrup, vegetable purée, liquid extract, liqueur, or nut or seed butter, combine with the custard and/or place in the bottom of the ramekins.

STEP 4

Divide custard mixture evenly among ramekins. Place the ramekins in a shallow roasting pan. Pour hot water into roasting pan to come halfway up sides of ramekins. Bake until custard barely moves when ramekins are shaken, or a knife inserted in the center of the custard comes out clean, about 45 to 60 minutes. Remove the ramekins from the roasting pan and let cool at room temperature for at least 45 minutes. Refrigerate for at least 4 hours (overnight is best).

STEP 5

Just before serving, sprinkle granulated sugar evenly over custards to cover completely. Turn upside down to remove excess sugar. For best results, ignite a blowtorch and caramelize sugar until evenly melted, moving the torch constantly so sugar doesn't burn. Alternatively, preheat the oven broiler to high. Broil cold custards close to element until sugar is caramelized and melted, about 2 to 3 minutes. Watch carefully to ensure sugar doesn't burn.

FRUITS & BERRIES

apple + nutmeg

key lime + ginger

orange + basil

fig + black pepper

pear + star anise

mandarin + cardamom

strawberry + licorice

NUTS & CHOCOLATE

chestnut + apple + vanilla

hazelnut + plum + cinnamon

walnut + maple butter

coconut + litchi + kaffir

chocolate + pecan + marshmallow

HERBS & SPICES

thyme + citrus zest

rosemary + grapefruit

lemongrass + pistachio

tamarind + banana

mint + cherry

lemon verbena + blueberry

lavender + peach

SWEET VEGETABLES

pumpkin + quince + mace

corn + pear + chicory

sweet potato + curry

carrot + anise seeds

parsnip + almond + vanilla

cassava + coconut milk

rhubarb + ginger + grenadine

boniato + garam masala

CHAPTER 9

Pairing Wine with Crème Brûlée

Food and wine pairing can be difficult. Not all sweet wines are dessert wines, and not every dessert should be matched with a sweet wine. However, if there is one dish upon which there is total consensus regarding wine pairing, it would have to be crème brûlée. Match the classic version of crème brûlée with a rich, sweet wine. This is almost foolproof. Pair crème brûlée with botrytis-affected wine—it's a match made in heaven.

Botrytis cinerea is a fungus that affects certain grape varietals resulting in what is known as "noble rot." The final result is a condition that yields distinctive and delicious sweet wines. Some of the best-known botrytis wines (which are ideal partners to crème brûlée) include *Tokaji Aszú* from Hungary, Sauternes from France, and *Beerenauslese* or *Trockenbeerenauslese* from Germany.

Custard-type desserts also pair well with other types of sweet wines such as Canadian icewine. This exceptional wine is made from grapes that are left on the vine well into the winter months. The resulting freezing and thawing of the grapes dehydrate the fruit and concentrate the sugars and acids in the grapes.

As a general pairing guideline, keep the following points in mind. However, the first rule about wine pairing is that there are no rules. Try different types of wines and keep notes; experimentation is the key to finding the best match.

CONTRAST: Look for sweet wines such as Vidal or Riesling icewine that have enough acidity to cut through the richness of custard-type desserts.

TRY BOTRYTIS: Select wines that have been affected by botrytis as they will possess those very compatible honeyed and caramelized notes such as Sauvignon, Sémillon Blanc, Sauternes, or Riesling Beerenauslese or Trockenbeerenauslese.

SIP WITH SAVORY: Consider dry white wines such as Chardonnay, Sauvignon Blanc, Pinot Blanc, or Pinot Gris or Grigio, and dry sparkling wines or Champagne with savory custards.

MATCH WEIGHT: Match the weight of the wine with that of the dessert. For example, richer chocolate custard may be better suited with richer fortified wines such as French Beaumes de Venise or Californian Black Muscat or perhaps even an LBV port.

READ TASTING NOTES: Read about the tasting notes of the wines and try to match or contrast them with the leading note of the custard. For example, we suggest Chenin Blanc for custards that also contain tree fruit. Try fortified

Muscat-based wines such as Liqueur Muscat or Liqueur Tokay from Australia, or Orange Muscat from France or California with custards made with nuts and spices. Or try wines such as French Vin de Paille or Italian Vin Santo with vegetable-based sweet custards.

LOOK FOR BALANCE: Look for balance between the wine and the food. Think about sweetness, acidity, and temperature since each of these can drastically influence how the wine will taste or stand against the food. Experiment with texture also. For example, try sweet sparkling wines such as Moscato d'Asti with lighter-textured custards.

Look for ingredients such as agar powder and xanthan gum at your local health food store. Results may vary depending on the brand.

For the best results, please go to DC DUBY Wild Sweets® Virtual Boutique (www.dcduby.com). We feature many specialty ingredients under the Elements line, including xanthan gum (XAGUM), agar powder (ARGUM), pectin powder (PECTO), and more.

Our website features cooking videos, including several crème brûlée recipes, along with techniques and tips from this book. We also offer cooking classes in the Wild Sweets Theatre. For more information or to purchase products or book a cooking class, visit the website or call (604) 277-6102.